Little Vegetarian Feasts

Main-Dish Salads

Martha Rose Shulman

Illustrated by Debbie Drechsler
Designed by B. W. Honeycutt
Produced by The Miller Press, Inc.

Bantam Books
NEW YORK • TORONTO • LONDON • SYDNEY • AUCKLAND

Little Vegetarian Feasts
Main-Dish Salads
A Bantam Book/September 1992

Library of Congress Cataloging-in-Publication Data

Shulman, Martha Rose.
Little vegetarian feasts. Main-dish salads/Martha Rose Shulman;
illustrations by Debbie Drechsler; designed by B.W. Honeycutt;
produced by The Miller Press, Inc.

p. cm.
ISBN 0-553-08570-0
1. Salads. I. Title
TX807.S58   1992
641.8′3 — dc20   91-46153
                                                                        CIP

Published simultaneously in the United States and Canada

Bantam Books are published by Bantam Books, a division of Bantam
Doubleday Dell Publishing Group, Inc. Its trademark, consisting of the
words "Bantam Books" and the portrayal of a rooster, is Registered in
U.S. Patent and Trademark Office and in other countries. Marca Registrada.
Bantam Books, 666 Fifth Avenue, New York, New York 10103.

Printed in THE UNITED STATES OF AMERICA
0   9   8   7   6   5   4   3   2   1

Main Dish Salads

Contents

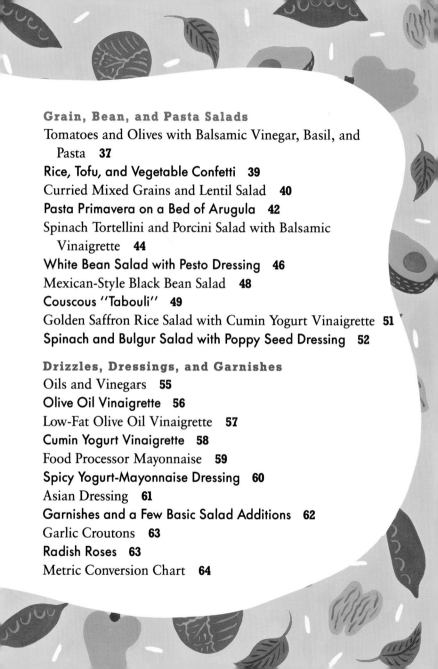

INTRODUCTION

What makes a salad a salad? The simple answer is salad
dressing, which can be more or less tangy, according to
your taste. Toss anything with a salad dressing and it's a
salad, whether it's a leaf, a vegetable, a fruit, an herb, an
edible flower, a grain, or a bean. Very simple ingredients
can be transformed into luscious salads, given a good
dressing with the right seasonings. If I have on hand a
bunch of broccoli, some eggs, and potatoes, I can steam
the broccoli and potatoes, make a sharp, mustardy
vinaigrette, soft-cook the egg, and toss everything together
in a bowl with a little slivered Parmesan, for an enticing
warm salad. Now *that* is a meal (and it happens to be one
of my favorite winter dinners).

Because salads require fresh ingredients, they are by
nature healthful to some degree. But they aren't
necessarily light. You can make a meal out of leafy greens,
but if they're swimming in oil, you'll be getting much more
fat than you need. In fact, salad dressings require only a
little bit of oil to carry the flavors, especially when you're
using tasty, high-quality oils and vinegars. The oils in most

dressings can be stretched with yogurt or buttermilk; good olive and walnut oils, especially, are so fragrant that they won't lose their character.

To expand your repertoire, here are three weeks' worth of exciting, envigorating main-dish salads, conceived for your pleasure and good health.

Salad Basics

Anyone can make a salad. No difficult techniques are required, and many of these recipes involve no cooking at all. Still, there are a few salad rules that should always be followed. *Imperative:*

1. Wash and dry lettuces, greens, and herbs thoroughly.
2. Toss leafy salads with just enough dressing to coat the leaves before serving.
3. Tear lettuces gently to avoid bruising. Use scissors to cut up fresh herbs.
4. Add bright green vegetables and herbs to dressed salads shortly before serving, unless instructed otherwise.

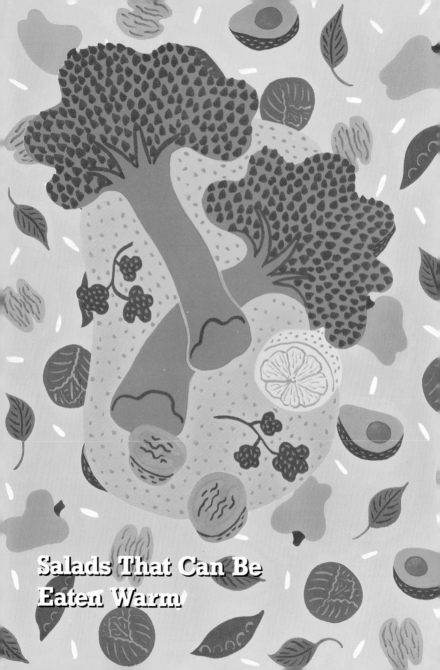

Salads That Can Be
Eaten Warm

Autumn Wild Rice, Walnut & Broccoli Salad

Serves 4 to 6

This nutty salad is a mainstay in my home. Naturally you could substitute other green vegetables for the broccoli, but the broccoli florets are particularly appealing because they absorb the flavors in the dressing. If you have vegetable stock, use that instead of water.

3½ cups water
1 cup wild rice, rinsed
salt to taste
1 pound broccoli florets, steamed until
    crisp-tender
½ cup broken walnut pieces or pecans, toasted
½ cup chopped fresh parsley
2 tablespoons fresh lemon juice
1 tablespoon red wine vinegar or sherry
    vinegar (or more to taste)
1 garlic clove, minced or put through a
    press (optional)
¼ cup plain low-fat yogurt
¼ cup walnut oil
freshly ground pepper to taste

1. Bring the water to a boil and add the rice. Add salt to taste, bring back to a boil, reduce the heat, cover, and simmmer for about 40 minutes, until the rice is tender. Drain and toss with the broccoli, nuts, and parsley.   →

2. Mix together the lemon juice, vinegar, garlic, and yogurt. Whisk in the walnut oil and add salt and pepper. Toss with the rice mixture, correct the seasonings, and serve; or refrigerate until shortly before serving.

Note: If the salad is to be refrigerated for a long time, add the broccoli and parsley shortly before serving to retain their bright color.

Potato Salad with Goat Cheese, Red Onions, and Sage

Serves 4 to 5

When goat cheese is tossed with hot potatoes it melts luxuriously around the potatoes. Fresh sage adds another dimension, to make an unforgettable meal.

> 2 pounds (8 medium-size) new or russet potatoes, scrubbed
> ¼ cup dry white wine
> 1 large *or* 2 small red onions, peeled and very thinly sliced
> ¼ cup finely chopped fresh parsley
> salt and freshly ground pepper to taste
> 3 ounces not-too-salty fresh goat cheese, cut into pieces or crumbled
> 2 tablespoons red wine vinegar (or more to taste)
> 1 teaspoon Dijon mustard (or more to taste)
> ¼ cup olive oil
> 2 tablespoons slivered fresh sage leaves (or more to taste)

1. Steam or boil the potatoes until tender. Remove from the heat and dice or slice while still warm. Transfer to a bowl and toss at once with the wine, red onions, parsley, and salt and pepper. Stir in the goat cheese.

2. Mix together the vinegar, mustard, and olive oil and combine well. Toss with the salad.

3. Shortly before serving, add the slivered sage leaves, toss together, and adjust seasonings. You may wish to add more mustard, vinegar, or salt. Serve warm or at room temperature.

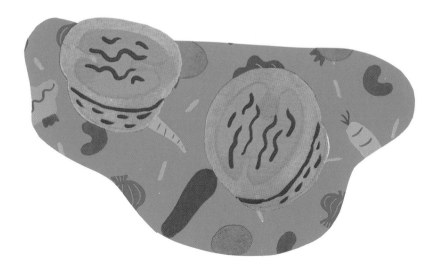

Gingery Buckwheat Noodle and Green Bean Salad

Buckwheat noodles have a seductive, fragrant, earthy flavor that is heightened here by the nutty, gingery dressing. The salad is good warm or cold.

¾ pound soba (buckwheat noodles, found
   in imported food stores)
6 ounces green beans, trimmed and cut into
   1-inch lengths (about 1½ cups)
2 tablespoons dark Chinese sesame oil
6 ounces firm tofu, sliced and sprinkled
   with soy sauce
¼ cup chopped cilantro (or more to taste)
2 tablespoons roasted sesame seeds
1 recipe Asian Dressing (page 61)

1. Bring a large pot of water to a boil and add a generous amount of salt. Add the soba noodles, cook for a minute or two, and add the green beans. Cook for another few minutes or until the soba is cooked al dente (some buckwheat noodles are thinner than others and thus cook faster).
2. Drain the noodles and toss with the sesame oil in a bowl.
3. Add the remaining ingredients, toss, and serve; or serve at room temperature or chilled.

Warm Broccoli and Potato Salad

This simple salad is quickly thrown together and makes a delightful winter meal.

> 1 pound (4 medium-size) new or russet potatoes, scrubbed
> 2 tablespoons dry white wine
> 2 tablespoons chopped fresh parsley
> salt and freshly ground pepper to taste
> 1 large (1½ to 2 pounds) bunch of broccoli, broken into florets, stems peeled and sliced
> 2 tablespoons fresh lemon juice
> 1 to 2 tablespoons red wine vinegar or sherry vinegar to taste
> 1 teaspoon Dijon mustard
> 1 small garlic clove, minced or put through a press
> 6 tablespoons plain low-fat yogurt
> ¼ cup olive oil
> 2 ounces Parmesan cheese, slivered

1. Steam or boil the potatoes until tender. Drain and cut into quarters or thick slices. Toss with the white wine, parsley, and salt and pepper.

2. Steam the broccoli until tender, about five to eight minutes. Meanwhile, make the dressing. Mix together the lemon juice, vinegar, mustard, garlic, and yogurt. Add salt and pepper to taste. Stir in the olive oil.

3. Drain the broccoli, refresh under cold water, and toss with the potatoes, dressing, and Parmesan. Serve warm.

Cellophane Noodle Salad with Vegetable Threads

Serves 4

Cellophane noodles, made from crushed mung beans, have a terrific chewy texture; they're like slippery pasta that never gets soggy. Also called bean threads, they're easily obtained in Asian food markets. This salad, seasoned with crushed coriander seeds, balsamic vinegar, and dark sesame oil, is good warm or chilled.

¼ pound cellophane noodles
1 large carrot, grated
½ large cucumber, peeled if waxed, grated
1 large green or red bell pepper, cut into very thin 1-inch-long slivers
4 scallions, both white and green parts, cut into slivers
¼ pound firm tofu, crumbled and sprinkled with soy sauce (optional)
½ cup chopped cilantro
1 tablespoon coriander seeds, crushed in a mortar and pestle
3 tablespoons balsamic vinegar
2 tablespoons dark Chinese sesame oil
¼ cup dark sesame oil
2 tablespoons tamari or Kikkoman soy sauce
salt if desired
lots of freshly ground pepper

1. Place the noodles in a bowl without removing the strings or rubber bands holding the skeins together. Pour on hot tap water to cover and let soak for about three minutes or until softened (some brands take longer than others). Drain, untie the skeins, and cut the skeins in half with scissors so that the noodles aren't too long.

2. Toss the noodles with the vegetables, tofu, cilantro, and coriander seeds.

3. Mix together the remaining ingredients and toss with the salad. Heat through for a few seconds (not more than 30 seconds, or the noodles will get too soft) in a nonstick skillet over medium-high heat. Serve warm or chilled. (Skip the skillet heating if you're serving the salad cold.)

Vegetable Salads

MixeD WiNteR LeTTuces, Apples, WalNuts, aNd RoquefoRt

**Opposites do attract. Here's a match made in heaven.
Note the play of dark and light colors, the sweet apples
and nutty dressing against the bitter greens, and the
crunchy walnuts and creamy cheese.**

> 1 pound Belgian endives
> 1 medium-size head of radicchio, leaves
>   separated and washed
> 1 small bunch of watercress, bottom of the
>   stems cut away, leaves and remaining
>   stems washed and dried
> 2 tart apples, cored and sliced
> 2 tablespoons fresh lemon juice
> ⅓ cup broken walnut pieces
> 6 ounces Roquefort cheese, crumbled (about
>   1½ cups)
> 2 tablespoons chopped fresh parsley
> 1 tablespoon balsamic vinegar
> 1 to 2 tablespoons sherry vinegar or red
>   wine vinegar to taste
> 1 teaspoon Dijon mustard
> salt and freshly ground pepper to taste
> ½ cup plain low-fat yogurt
> 3 tablespoons walnut oil

→

19

1. Wash the endives and pat them dry. Either cut them into thick slices or separate the leaves. If the leaves still are wet, dry them. Toss them together with the radicchio and watercress.

2. Toss the apples with one tablespoon of the lemon juice. Add to the greens along with the walnuts, cheese, and parsley. Chill if not serving right away.

3. Mix together the vinegars, remaining lemon juice, mustard, and salt and pepper. Whisk in the yogurt and walnut oil. Toss with the salad just before serving.

HOW TO WASH LETTUCE, SPINACH, AND OTHER GREENS

Fill one half of a double sink, a large bowl, or the bottom part of your salad spinner with cold water. Remove the tough outer leaves of lettuces and the stems from spinach. Run each leaf briefly under the tap, then place in the water to soak for a few minutes. Swish the leaves around in the water, then lift the leaves out of the soaking water. Drain the soaking water, fill the sink or bowl again, and swish the leaves around again. If the stems of the leaves are still sandy, take each leaf and run it under the faucet. Holding the base of the leaf under the faucet, briskly rub between your thumb and forefinger to remove tenacious grit. Look closely to make sure all the dirt is removed. With spinach the dirt will often be caked on the leaves, so you have to rinse spinach more than once. Lift the leaves out of the water (don't just drain, because the dirt in the water will settle back on the leaves) and rinse once more. Now dry the leaves in batches in a salad spinner. If you're not using the greens right away, place them in a plastic bag or wrap in a clean dish towel, place in a plastic bag, and seal. Refrigerate until shortly before using.

Salad herbs should be rinsed and swished briefly in water. Once is usually enough. Blot with paper towels to dry.

CReaMY CucuMbeR aNd Feta Cheese Salad

Serve this uncomplicated, creamy, addictive salad with black bread or pita and sliced tomatoes on the side. I like it best seasoned simply, with salt and a generous amount of pepper.

1 long European cucumber, washed and
    finely chopped, *or* 2 medium-size
    ordinary cucumbers, peeled if waxed,
    washed, seeded, and finely chopped
salt to taste
2 cups *fromage blanc* (see note), *or* 1½ cups
    low-fat cottage cheese blended until
    smooth with ½ cup plain low-fat yogurt
6 ounces feta cheese, crumbled (about 1 cup)
1 small red onion, very thinly sliced
    (optional)
1 or 2 garlic cloves, pounded to a puree in a
    mortar and pestle or put through a press
    (optional)
1 to 2 tablespoons chopped fresh mint or
    oregano (optional)
freshly ground pepper to taste

1. Toss the cucumber with a generous amount of salt and let sit in a colander for 30 minutes. Rinse briefly and pat dry.
2. Stir together the *fromage blanc* or cottage cheese/yogurt mixture and the feta cheese. Toss with the cucumbers in a →

bowl. Add the onion, garlic, and herbs as desired, lots of freshly ground pepper, and salt to taste.

3. Chill until ready to serve.

Note: Fromage blanc is a smooth-textured fermented milk product, which tastes kind of like a cross between cottage cheese and yogurt. It comes in very low-fat versions. You can find it in some supermarkets and healthfood stores. You can make something that resembles fromage blanc by blending three parts cottage cheese and one part plain low-fat yogurt together until smooth.

Potato-Egg Salad with Fresh Peas

Serves 4 to 6

Here is a lighter, more lively and colorful version of traditional American potato salad.

2 pounds (8 medium-size) new or russet
   potatoes, scrubbed
¼ cup dry white wine
salt and freshly ground pepper to taste
4 to 5 tablespoons vinegar: sherry, red
   wine, or white wine
1 heaped tablespoon Dijon mustard
½ cup chopped fresh parsley
⅓ cup food processor mayonnaise (page 59)
½ cup plain low-fat yogurt
fresh lemon juice to taste
2 celery ribs, chopped
1 medium-size red onion, chopped
1 medium-size red bell pepper, diced

1 cup fresh or frozen peas, steamed until tender
4 hard-cooked eggs, chopped

1. Steam or boil the potatoes until tender. Remove from the heat and slice or dice while still hot (use a towel to steady them with one hand while you cut with the other). Toss at once with the white wine, salt and pepper, vinegar, mustard, and half the parsley. Allow to cool; then refrigerate for an hour.

2. Mix together the mayonnaise and yogurt. Add salt, pepper, and lemon juice to taste. Toss with the potatoes and the remaining ingredients, adjust the seasoning, and serve.

LEAFY GREENS

Soft, Delicate Lettuces
Bibb, butter, or Boston lettuce
Oak leaf lettuce (red and green, slightly bitter)
Red leaf lettuce

Slightly Crunchy Lettuces
Romaine lettuce
Leaf lettuce

Hearty, Bitter Lettuces
(Good with nutty dressings and sweet vinegars.)
Escarole
Curly endive (also known as frisée)
Belgian endive
Red and green chicory
Radicchio

Sweet Greens
Spinach

Peppery, Pungent, and Bitter Greens
Watercress (peppery)
Arugula or rocket (peppery/pungent)
Nasturtium leaves (pungent)
Sorrel (very acidic/pungent; also considered an herb)
Radish tops (pungent)
Beet and mustard greens (pungent; young ones are best)
Dandelion greens (bitter)
Swiss chard (slightly bitter)

Hard-Leafed Cabbages
Round-headed red and white or green cabbage

Softer-Leafed Cabbages
Savoy cabbage
Napa or Chinese cabbage

Bean Sprout Salad
with Spicy Peanut Dressing

**This isn't an authentic version of the peanutty
Indonesian salad called gado-gado, because it's not as
rich (no coconut). But all the lively flavors are there—
ginger, peanuts, chili, lime—it's irresistible.**

1⅛ cups water
8 cups (1 pound) bean sprouts (soybean or
     mung bean)
¼ cup chopped fresh mint
¼ cup chopped cilantro (or more to taste)
1 red bell pepper, cut into thin strips about
     1-inch long
½ pound firm tofu, cut into slivers and
     sprinkled with soy sauce
juice of 1 large lemon
6 tablespoons crunchy peanut butter
1 to 2 teaspoons grated or finely chopped
     fresh ginger to taste
1 garlic clove, minced or put through a press
1 teaspoon mild-flavored honey, such as
     clover or acacia
½ teaspoon chili powder (or more to taste)
salt and cayenne pepper to taste
2 teaspoons cider vinegar
2 tablespoons fresh lime juice
leaf lettuce for serving (optional)
3 tablespoons chopped or coarsely ground
     roasted peanuts
fresh mint sprigs for garnish

1. Heat six tablespoons of the water in a large frying pan and add the bean sprouts. Cook over medium-high heat for one minute, drain, and transfer to a bowl. Allow to cool for a few minutes. Add the mint, cilantro, red bell pepper, and tofu and toss together with the lemon juice.

2. In a saucepan, mix together the peanut butter, ginger, garlic, honey, chili powder, salt and cayenne pepper, remaining ¾ cup water, and vinegar. Heat through, stirring, until the mixture is smooth. Add the lime juice and adjust the seasonings. Toss with the salad. Line a bowl or platter with lettuce leaves if you wish and top with the salad. Sprinkle on the roasted peanuts and serve garnished with sprigs of fresh mint.

CuRLY ENdive Salad with Tofu "LaRdoNs"

This is based on the traditional French curly endive (frisée) salad with bacon and croutons and poached eggs.

½ pound firm tofu
1 tablespoon tamari or Kikkoman soy sauce
2 tablespoons olive oil
1 garlic clove, minced or put through a press
1 large head of curly endive, tough outer
  leaves removed, remaining leaves washed
  thoroughly and dried
1 cup diced garlic croutons (page 63)
1 tablespoon lightly toasted pine nuts
about ½ cup chopped fresh herbs, such as
  parsley, chervil, tarragon, chives, basil
1 recipe Low-Fat Olive Oil Vinaigrette (page
  57), sharpened with a little extra vinegar
  if you wish
4 medium-size eggs, poached (can be warm
  or room temperature)

1. To firm up the tofu, wrap it in a towel and place under a cutting board for 30 minutes. Cut it into ½-inch cubes (or a little smaller). Toss with the soy sauce and sauté in the olive oil in a nonstick frying pan until browned and crisp on the edges. Remove from the heat and toss with the garlic.

2. Toss all of the ingredients except the eggs with the vinaigrette. Divide among four salad plates; top each portion with a poached egg. Or serve in a wide salad bowl with the poached eggs on top of the salad.

Spicy Eggplant and Tofu Salad

Serves 4

All kinds of luscious textures and flavors come together in this pungent salad: rich, smooth, savory eggplant; delicate tofu; crunchy, bright snow peas; and juicy, sweet red pepper.

> 1 large (1 to 1½ pound) eggplant, cut in half lengthwise
> ¾ pound firm tofu, sliced and sprinkled with tamari or Kikkoman soy sauce
> ¼ pound snow peas, steamed until crisp-tender
> 4 scallions, both white and green parts, thinly sliced
> 1 small red bell pepper, thinly sliced
> ¼ cup chopped cilantro
> dash of hot red pepper flakes
> 1 recipe Asian Dressing (page 61)

1. Preheat the oven to 450 degrees. Score the cut sides of the eggplant halves down the middle, being careful not to pierce the skin, and place cut side down on a lightly oiled baking sheet. Bake for 30 minutes, until the skins are shriveled and the eggplant cooked through. Remove from the heat and allow to cool. When cool enough to handle, cut into ¼-inch slices and transfer to a bowl. Add the tofu, remaining vegetables, cilantro, and red pepper flakes.

2. Toss the dressing with the eggplant mixture and serve; or chill until ready to serve.

Spinach Salad with Pears, Pecans, and Feta

Spinach, feta, mint, and pecans—an inspired combination of Middle Eastern tastes with the unusual addition of pears.

10 ounces fresh spinach, stems removed and
  leaves washed
2 large ripe but firm pears, peeled, cored,
  and sliced
¼ cup chopped pecans
¼ pound feta cheese, crumbled (about ⅔ cup)
2 tablespoons chopped fresh mint
2 tablespoons fresh lemon juice
1 tablespoon sherry vinegar or champagne
  vinegar
1 teaspoon mild-flavored honey, such as
  clover or acacia
½ to 1 teaspoon Dijon mustard to taste
¼ cup plain low-fat yogurt
¼ cup olive oil
salt and freshly ground pepper to taste

1. Toss together the spinach, pears, pecans, feta, and mint.
2. Mix together the lemon juice, vinegar, honey, mustard, and yogurt. Whisk in the olive oil or shake together in a jar. Add salt and pepper. Toss with the salad just before serving.

Note: If you are preparing this salad ahead of time, toss the sliced pears with a tablespoon or two of lemon juice so they don't discolor.

Sweet and Sour Red Peppers, Eggplant, and White Beans

This glistening, sweet and tangy mixture is inspired by Middle Eastern dishes, but traditional versions would be swimming in olive oil.

1 pound (1 large) eggplant, cut in half
   lengthwise
3 cups water
¼ cup mild-flavored honey, such as clover
   or acacia, or sugar
½ teaspoon salt
1 medium-size onion, sliced
4 large garlic cloves, sliced (optional)
½ cup good-quality sherry vinegar or
   champagne vinegar
1 bay leaf
1 large red bell pepper, cut into strips about
   2-inches long by 1-inch wide
1 14-ounce can white beans, drained (1½
   cups cooked beans)
1 tablespoon slivered fresh mint leaves, plus
   fresh mint sprigs for garnish
additional salt and freshly ground pepper to taste
lettuce leaves for serving

1. Preheat the oven to 450 degrees. Score the eggplants on the cut side and place them cut side down on a lightly oiled baking sheet. Bake for 20 minutes. Remove from the heat, remove the skin if desired when cool enough to handle, and cut into 1-inch chunks.

2. Meanwhile, combine the water, honey or sugar, salt, onion, garlic, vinegar, and bay leaf in a large noncorrodible saucepan and bring to a boil. Add the peppers and cook over medium-high heat for 15 minutes. Add the eggplant and cook for another five minutes or until cooked through.

3. Drain the vegetables and transfer to a bowl, reserving the liquid. Add the beans, mint, and salt and pepper. Allow to cool. Return the cooking liquid to the pot and bring to a fast boil. Reduce to one cup. Pour over the vegetables, cover, and refrigerate.

4. To serve, line a platter, bowl, or plates with lettuce leaves and top with the vegetable mixture. Garnish with additional fresh mint sprigs.

Tomatoes, Mozzarella, Avocado, Zucchini and Its Flowers

This brightly colored elaboration on the traditional Italian tomato and mozzarella salad features both zucchini and zucchini blossoms — if they're available. Needless to say, sweet ripe tomatoes are essential.

1 pound small zucchini, very thinly sliced
a couple of handfuls of zucchini blossoms if available
½ pound mozzarella cheese, very thinly sliced
3 tablespoons fresh lemon juice
¼ cup olive oil
1 tablespoon chopped fresh chives
coarse salt and freshly ground pepper to taste
1½ pounds (6 medium-size) ripe red tomatoes, sliced
2 tablespoons balsamic vinegar
1 garlic clove, minced or put through a press (optional)
8 large fresh basil leaves, cut into slivers (or more to taste)
1 avocado, peeled, pitted, and sliced

1. Combine the zucchini, zucchini blossoms, and half the mozzarella in a bowl. Mix together the lemon juice, olive oil, and chives and add salt and pepper. Toss with the zucchini mixture. Place in the middle of a platter.

2. Combine the tomatoes, balsamic vinegar, coarse salt and pepper, garlic if desired, and basil and gently toss together in a bowl. Add the remaining mozzarella and the avocado slices and surround the zucchini with this mixture. Drizzle all the juices remaining in the bowl over the tomatoes, avocados, and mozzarella. Grind on some pepper and serve.

Vegetables and Fava Beans Vinaigrette

I like to serve huge platters of this wonderful salad for parties. I always make more than I need so that I can have terrific instant meals on hand in the refrigerator for the next few days (try packing leftovers into pita bread).

1 pound (4 medium-size) new potatoes, scrubbed, steamed or boiled until crisp-tender, and either sliced ½-inch thick or quartered

½ head of cauliflower, broken into florets and steamed for five minutes

½ pint cherry tomatoes (a combination of red and yellow is nice)

1 red bell pepper, cut into 1-inch squares or rings

1 green bell pepper, cut into 1-inch squares or rings

½ long European *or* 1 ordinary cucumber, peeled if waxed and sliced

½ pound (about 15) medium-size mushrooms, stems removed, caps rinsed and dried

1 red onion, sliced into rings

a handful of imported black olives, such as Kalamata or Nyons, pitted if desired

1½ cups cooked (½ cup dried) giant white (fava) beans

a double batch of Low-Fat Olive Oil Vinaigrette (page 57)

¼ pound feta cheese, crumbled (about ⅔
   cup; optional)
½ cup chopped fresh herbs, such as
   tarragon, parsley, basil, dill, chervil,
   chives, sage
lettuce leaves (optional), radish roses (page 63),
   and fresh herb sprigs for garnish

1. Place all of the prepared vegetables in a bowl with the olives and beans. Toss with the vinaigrette, the feta if desired, and half the chopped fresh herbs. Cover and refrigerate for at least one hour.

2. Shortly before serving, toss the vegetable mixture with the remaining herbs and adjust the seasonings.

3. Line a platter or salad bowl with the lettuce leaves if desired and top with the vegetables. Decorate with radish roses and sprigs of fresh herbs and serve.

Grain, Bean, and Pasta Salads

Tomatoes and Olives with Balsamic Vinegar, Basil, and Pasta

Serves 4

Take this salad to a picnic on a hot summer night. I don't like to call it a pasta salad, because the tomatoes are the real focus. But if you get ripe red juicy ones, which are essential, you need some pasta to catch the marvelous juice. This salad is good warm, at room temperature or chilled.

2 pounds (8 medium-size) sweet ripe
   tomatoes, peeled if desired and cut into wedges
12 to 16 black Nyons or Niçoise olives,
   pitted if desired
6 ounces mozzarella cheese, cut into thin slices
salt and freshly ground pepper to taste
2 garlic cloves, minced or put through a press
3 tablespoons balsamic vinegar
3 tablespoons olive oil
3 tablespoons torn-up or cut-up basil leaves
6 ounces orecchiette, small pasta shells,
   or fusilli

1. Toss the tomatoes, olives, mozzarella, salt and pepper, and garlic together in a bowl with the vinegar and olive oil. Add the basil unless you're not serving right away, in which case add it no more than 30 minutes before serving.   →

2. Cook the pasta al dente in a large pot of salted boiling water. Drain and toss with the tomato mixture. Adjust the seasonings and serve immediately, or refrigerate until shortly before serving.

GRAINS, BEANS, AND PASTA

Quick-Cooking Grains
Bulgur, couscous (bulgur and couscous are soaked and reconstituted rather than cooked), quinoa, basmati rice.

Longer-Cooking Grains
(30 minutes to an hour): Rice (white and brown), millet, kasha, wild rice, wheat berries, triticale.

Quick-Cooking Beans
(don't require soaking): lentils, black-eyed peas.

Longer-Cooking Beans
(require soaking and at least 1 hour of cooking; then again, you could use canned beans if you don't need the cooking liquid for the dressing): Black beans, chick peas, fava beans (giant white), pinto beans, white beans (navy, great northern, small white).

Pasta
Shapes like fusilli, penne, orecchiette, and macaroni are best. Ravioli and tortellini also make great salads. Asian pastas include buckwheat noodles (soba), rice noodles or vermicelli, and cellophane noodles.

Rice, Tofu, and Vegetable Confetti

Serves 6

Serve this gaily speckled mixture for a party. It looks particularly festive for New Year's Eve.

1½ cups brown rice, cooked
¼ cup fresh lemon juice
1 red bell pepper, finely diced
1 green bell pepper, finely diced
6 radishes, thinly sliced
6 scallions, thinly sliced or chopped
1 cup fresh or thawed frozen peas, steamed
    for 5 minutes and refreshed under cold water
½ cup chopped fresh parsley
¼ to ⅓ cup other chopped fresh herbs, such
    as tarragon, basil, chervil, chives, fennel,
    thyme to taste
¼ pound firm tofu, sprinkled with tamari
    or Kikkoman soy sauce and finely diced
½ cup (2 ounces) freshly grated Parmesan cheese
1 recipe Olive Oil Vinaigrette (page 56) or
    Low-Fat Olive Oil Vinaigrette (page 57)
leaf lettuce for serving (optional)
garnishes: radish roses (page 63), cherry
    tomatoes or tomato wedges, and imported
    black olives for garnish

1. Toss the rice with the lemon juice, vegetables, herbs, tofu, and Parmesan. Add the dressing, toss again, and adjust the seasonings. →

2. Pack the salad into a well-oiled ring mold or bowl and chill for an hour or more. Line a platter with lettuce leaves if desired. Dip the mold into warm water for a few minutes, then unmold onto the platter. Decorate with the garnishes of your choice (if you've made a ring, fill it with cherry tomatoes) and serve.

Curried Mixed Grains and Lentil Salad

Serves 6 to 8

Here's a great way to introduce a range of grains and legumes into your diet. This substantial salad is bursting with texture and color.

> 1 cup brown rice, rinsed
> ¾ cup wheat berries, rinsed
> ½ cup lentils, rinsed and picked over
> 2 tablespoons chopped chives
> 1 small green bell pepper, diced
> ½ long European cucumber *or* 1 small
>   ordinary cucumber, peeled if waxed,
>   seeded and diced
> 1½ cups Spicy Yogurt-Mayonnaise Dressing
>   (page 60)
> 6 ounces (about 1½ cups) snow peas or
>   green beans, blanched or steamed until
>   crisp-tender and cut into 1-inch lengths
> 3 tablespoons lemon juice (or to taste; optional)
> 6 tablespoons chopped cilantro or parsley
> cherry tomatoes for garnish

1. Cook the brown rice, the wheat berries, and the lentils separately (see note). Drain and toss together in a bowl. Allow to cool.

2. Toss the grains and beans with the remaining ingredients except the snow peas, lemon juice, cilantro, and cherry tomatoes. Cover and refrigerate for an hour or longer.

3. Shortly before serving, toss with the snow peas, lemon juice if desired, and ¼ cup of the cilantro. Sprinkle the remaining two tablespoons cilantro over the top, garnish with cherry tomatoes, and serve.

Note: To cook the brown rice, combine with two cups water and ¼ teaspoon salt in a saucepan. Bring to a boil, reduce heat, and cover. Simmer for 35 to 45 minutes, until the water is absorbed.

To cook the wheat berries, combine with three cups water and ¼ teaspoon salt, bring to a boil, reduce heat, cover, and cook for 50 minutes or until tender. Drain.

To cook the lentils, combine with a whole onion and one tablespoon vinegar in three cups water, bring to a boil, reduce heat, cover, and simmer for 40 minutes. Add ½ teaspoon of salt halfway through the cooking. Drain and discard the onion.

Pasta Primavera on a Bed of Arugula

Serves 6

What's new about this pasta salad? A bed of peppery arugula to set it off. And a sweet and garlicky sauce made from roasted red peppers, ripe tomatoes, and balsamic vinegar. People are completely crazy about this salad.

2 large (about 1 pound), red bell peppers
   roasted, peeled, and thinly sliced
3 to 4 large garlic cloves, minced or put
   through a press
2 tablespoons balsamic vinegar
salt to taste
1½ pounds (6 medium-size) ripe fresh
   tomatoes, peeled and diced
freshly ground pepper to taste
½ cup fresh basil leaves, torn up or cut into
   slivers, plus additional leaves for garnish
3 tablespoons olive oil
¾ pound fusilli
1 pound (1 cup shelled) fresh peas, steamed
   for 5 minutes, or 1 cup thawed frozen
6 tablespoons freshly grated Parmesan
6 ounces (about 2 cups) arugula, washed
   and trimmed

1. Toss the roasted peppers with one of the garlic cloves, one tablespoon of the vinegar, and salt to taste. Cover and marinate for at least one hour in or out of the refrigerator. Add the tomatoes, two more garlic cloves, salt and pepper to taste, the remaining tablespoon of balsamic vinegar, a tablespoon of the slivered basil leaves, and the olive oil. Cover if not using right away; marinate for up to a day in the refrigerator.

2. Cook the fusilli al dente in a large pot of salted boiling water. Drain and toss with the peppers and tomatoes and all their accumulated juice, the peas, Parmesan, remaining slivered basil, and more salt and pepper to taste. Taste and add more garlic if desired.

3. Line plates or a platter with arugula and top with the pasta mixture. Garnish with basil leaves and serve.

ROASTED SWEET RED BELL PEPPERS

There are several ways to roast the peppers. You can place them directly in a gas flame or below a broiler. Or you can place them in a dry skillet over an electric or gas burner or in a baking dish in a 450-degree oven. You want all the skin to blister and blacken. Keep turning the peppers until they are uniformly charred, then place them in a plastic bag or a tightly covered bowl until cool enough to handle.

Peel off the blackened skin, split in half over a bowl (to retain the juice), and remove and discard the seeds and inner membranes. Rinse quickly under cool water and pat dry. Cut the halved peppers in half lengthwise, then into thin strips or small dice. Place in a bowl or serving dish and toss with a few tablespoons of olive oil, some minced garlic if you wish, and salt to taste. Cover and refrigerate. The peppers will keep for 5 days in the refrigerator.

Spinach Tortellini & Porcini Salad with Balsamic Vinaigrette

Can words describe this salad? It's exquisite, sensuous, deeply satisfying. The tortellini, dried porcini, and everything else combine marvelously with the sweet and garlicky vinaigrette. This salad is good warm or at room temperature.

1 ounce (1 cup) dried porcini
boiling water to cover
2 tablespoons balsamic vinegar
1 large garlic clove, minced or put through
   a press
¼ cup olive oil
salt and freshly ground pepper to taste
1 pound spinach and ricotta tortellini
½ cup fresh or thawed frozen peas
½ to ⅔ cup chopped fresh parsley *or* a
   mixture of parsley and basil
2 tablespoons slivered fresh sage leaves
2 ounces Parmesan cheese, either grated (½
   cup) or cut into thin slivers
¼ pound fresh spinach, stems removed and
   leaves washed, for garnish

1. Place the dried mushrooms in a bowl and pour on boiling water to cover. Let sit for 15 to 30 minutes, until the mushrooms are tender. Drain through a cheesecloth- or paper towel-lined strainer, reserving the liquid, and rinse the mushrooms thoroughly in several changes of water, making sure all the grit is washed away. Squeeze dry and chop coarsely if the mushrooms are very large.

2. Mix together the balsamic vinegar, garlic, olive oil, 2 tablespoons of the reserved mushroom soaking liquid, and salt and pepper to taste. (Set aside the remaining mushroom liquid to use in soups and sauces.)

3. Bring a large pot of water to a boil and add a tablespoon or so of salt. Add the tortellini and fresh peas (thawed frozen peas can be thrown into the water just before you drain the tortellini). Cook al dente, drain, and toss with the salad dressing, herbs, and Parmesan.

4. Line a salad bowl or platter with the spinach leaves, top with the salad, and serve.

White Bean Salad with Pesto Dressing

Pasta isn't the only vehicle for pesto, that luxurious basil puree. This simple salad is a delightful alternative. It's great for parties and will surprise and please your guests.

1 pound (2¼ cups) dried white beans,
    washed, picked over, and soaked
    overnight or for 6 hours
1 small onion, chopped
5 large garlic cloves, minced or put through
    a press
6 cups water
1 bay leaf
salt and freshly ground pepper to taste
2 cups tightly packed, fresh basil leaves
⅓ cup olive oil
½ cup (2 ounces) freshly grated Parmesan cheese
radish roses (page 63) or cherry tomatoes
    for garnish

1. Drain the beans and combine them in a large saucepan or soup pot with the onion, three of the garlic cloves, the water, and the bay leaf. Bring to a boil, reduce the heat, cover, and simmer for 1½ hours or until the beans are tender but not mushy. Add a teaspoon of salt (or more to taste) halfway through the cooking.

2. Drain the beans and reserve a cup of the cooking liquid.

3. In a mortar and pestle, a food processor, or a blender,

puree the basil leaves with the remaining garlic and about ¼ teaspoon salt. Add about ¼ cup of the bean cooking liquid, and slowly add the olive oil. Stir in the Parmesan and add lots of pepper. Thin, if you wish, with more of the cooking liquid from the beans.

4. Toss the pesto with the beans, transfer to an attractive bowl, and garnish with radish roses or cherry tomatoes. Serve warm or at room temperature.

Note: If you aren't serving this right away, allow it to come to room temperature before serving. Reheat a small amount of cooking liquid from the beans and toss with the salad.

FRESH HERBS

Sweet, Pungent, and Minty Herbs

Basil (sweet)
Chervil (sweet, delicate, and slightly pungent)
Chives (sweet, oniony)
Cilantro (fresh coriander; pungent)
Dill (sweet/pungent)
Fennel (sweet, anisy)
Mint (pennyroyal, peppermint, spearmint; peppermint is, yes, the most peppery)
Tarragon (sweet, pungent)

Savory and Bitter Herbs

Lovage (celerylike)
Marjoram (savory/bitter)
Oregano (savory/bitter)
Parsley (savory/bitter; flat-leaf is the tastiest)
Rosemary (savory/pungent)
Thyme and lemon thyme (savory/pungent)
Sage (savory/pungent; one of my favorites)

Mexican-Style Black Bean Salad

This is one of the best ways I can think of to make a meal out of beans. The salad is always a hit.

1 pound (2¼ cups) dried black beans, picked over, washed, and soaked overnight or for 6 hours
1 medium-size onion, chopped
5 large garlic cloves, minced or put through a press
2 quarts water
salt to taste
juice of 1 large lemon (¼ cup)
5 tablespoons red wine vinegar
1 heaped teaspoon Dijon mustard
1 teaspoon ground cumin (or more to taste)
¼ cup sunflower oil
1 medium-size green bell pepper, chopped
1 medium-size red bell pepper, chopped
½ cup chopped cilantro, plus cilantro sprigs for garnish

1. Drain the soaked beans and combine them with the onion, two garlic cloves, and the water in a large soup pot. Bring to a boil, reduce the heat, cover, and cook for one hour or until the beans are just about tender. Add salt (a teaspoon or more) and two more garlic cloves, and continue to cook for 30 to 60 minutes longer, until the beans are tender. Drain and reserve one cup of the cooking liquid.

2. Combine the lemon juice, vinegar, remaining garlic, Dijon mustard, and cumin and mix well. Whisk in the oil and the bean cooking liquid. Taste and adjust seasonings and toss the dressing with the beans. Refrigerate for several hours. Toss the beans with the peppers and cilantro shortly before serving. Serve garnished with cilantro.

CouScouS "TaBouLi"

Serves 6

In France there's a couscous salad called *tabouli*, though it's nothing like the tabouli you find in the Middle East. Still, it's lemony and good.

1½ cups couscous
1 cup fresh lemon juice
½ cup water
salt and freshly ground pepper to taste
¼ to ½ teaspoon ground cumin to taste
1 garlic clove, minced or put through a press
1 large bunch of fresh parsley, finely
    chopped (about 2 cups)
½ cup fresh mint leaves finely chopped (or
    more to taste)
4 scallions, both white and green parts,
    finely chopped (optional)
1 medium-size red bell pepper, diced
¾ to 1 pound (4 medium-size) tomatoes,
    peeled if desired, seeded and chopped   →

1 14-ounce can (2 cups) chick-peas, drained
  and rinsed
2 tablespoons olive oil
inner leaves from a head of romaine lettuce
  for garnish and to use as scoops

1. Place the couscous in a bowl and pour on the lemon juice and water. If the couscous isn't covered, add a little more water. Allow to sit and absorb the moisture, rubbing the couscous between your fingers every so often so that it doesn't clump together. It should be softened (with a slight degree of crunchiness) and fluffy in 15 to 20 minutes. Add salt and pepper.

2. Meanwhile, prepare the remaining ingredients. Add all the ingredients except the lettuce leaves to the couscous and toss together. Adjust the seasonings, cover, and refrigerate until ready to serve. Serve garnished with the romaine lettuce leaves.

Golden Saffron Rice Salad with Cumin Yogurt Vinaigrette

Serves 4

Saffron and cumin are the secrets to this exotic, brightly colored nourishing mélange. The salad can be made several hours ahead, then tossed shortly before serving.

2 cups water
1 cup long-grain white rice
¼ teaspoon saffron threads
¼ teaspoon salt
1 red bell pepper, cut into thin strips
4 scallions, both white and green parts,
  thinly sliced
⅓ long European *or* ½ ordinary cucumber,
  peeled, seeded, and chopped (about 1 cup)
6 ounces (1½ cups) green beans, trimmed
  and blanched
2 tablespoons pine nuts, toasted
3 ounces Monterey Jack or sharp Cheddar
  cheese, cut into ¼-inch cubes (optional)
¼ cup chopped cilantro
1 recipe Cumin Yogurt Vinaigrette (page 58)
radishes, sliced tomatoes, and black olives
  for garnish

1. Bring the water to a boil and add the rice, saffron, and salt. Reduce the heat, cover, and simmer until cooked al dente, about 20 to 25 minutes. Remove from the heat, →

drain off excess water, and allow to cool.

2. Toss the rice with the vegetables, pine nuts, cheese, and cilantro. Add the dressing and toss again. If you are holding the salad for several hours, keep the green beans and half the cilantro separate and toss with the salad shortly before serving.

3. Serve in an attractive bowl or on a platter, garnished with radishes, sliced tomatoes, and black olives.

Spinach and Bulgur Salad with Poppy Seed Dressing

Serves 6

Poppy seeds add crunch and a mysterious flavor to salads. This sweet-and-sour mixture looks especially pretty presented on a bed of red cabbage leaves.

1½ cups bulgur
¼ teaspoon salt
2½ cups boiling water
½ pound spinach, stems removed and leaves
    washed, dried, and chopped
¼ pound firm tofu, crumbled
1 tablespoon chopped fresh mint
whole red cabbage leaves for serving
For the Dressing:
2 tablespoons fresh lemon juice
2 tablespoons vinegar: sherry, red wine, or cider

2 tablespoons mild-flavored honey, such as
    clover or acacia
2 tablespoons poppy seeds
salt and freshly ground pepper to taste
⅔ cup plain low-fat yogurt
1 tablespoon sunflower oil

1. Place the bulgur in a bowl, mix with the salt, and pour on the boiling water. Let sit for 30 minutes or until the water is absorbed and the bulgur is soft. Drain and squeeze out any excess water in a towel. Allow to cool a little and toss with the spinach, tofu, and mint.

2. Mix together all the dressing ingredients and blend well. Toss with the bulgur-spinach mixture. Adjust the seasoning and chill until ready to serve.

3. Line a salad bowl, platter, or individual plates with red cabbage leaves. Top with the salad and serve.

MAKING YOUR OWN VINEGAR

You need a *mère* to make vinegar. A *mère* is a viscous cloud that develops in any bottle of vinegar after a few weeks or months. It is the equivalent of a yogurt starter. Pour off some of this *mère* into a wine bottle, a jug, or a special ceramic or glass bottle called a *vinaigrier*, and cover it with red or white wine. In a week you'll have vinegar. Every time you have wine left over from a dinner party—red, white, rosé, whatever—pour it into the jug. Homemade vinegar tends to be strong and robust.

Drizzles, Dressings, and Garnishes

Oils and Vinegars

The higher the quality of your oils and vinegars, the better your salad dressing will be.

Olive Oil: Use only virgin or extra-virgin olive oil—oils from the first pressing. Extra-virgin oils are the most aromatic (and expensive). These recipes use relatively little oil, so even a strongly flavored one won't overpower the other flavors in a dressing.

Walnut Oil: The best walnut oil comes from France. Walnut oil is so fragrant, just a couple of tablespoons are necessary for a rich, nutty salad. It goes especially well with bitter lettuces like endive (Belgian and curly), chicory, dandelion greens, and escarole. Keep this fragile oil in the refrigerator.

Hazelnut Oil: This is another nutty, fragrant fragile oil.

Peanut Oil: The most fragrant comes from China and is good in Asian dressings. I find it too strong for vinaigrette, but refined peanut oil has a neutral flavor and can be used for vinaigrettes and mayonnaise.

Canola or Sunflower Oil: These neutral-flavored oils are used for mayonnaise and some vinaigrettes.

Safflower Oil: Another mild-flavored oil, although I find it stronger than sunflower oil, with which it can be used interchangeably.

Dark Sesame Oil: A Chinese oil made from roasted sesame seeds. Very nutty and fragrant; a little goes a long way. It's a marvelous seasoning, great in Asian dressings.

Mild Vinegars: Champagne, rice wine, cider, and tarragon vinegars are all in this category with low acidity.

Robust Vinegars: Aged red wine vinegar and sherry vinegar (this is not as strong as red wine vinegar) have a more assertive flavor.

Sweet Vinegar: Balsamic vinegar. Terrific with tomatoes, bitter greens, and in Asian dressings.

Herb-Flavored Oils and Vinegars: Place sprigs of fresh herbs—such as tarragon, basil, dill, thyme, rosemary, or mint—in clean, dry bottles and fill with vinegar or olive oil.

Garlic, Shallot or Hot Pepper-Flavored Oil: You can also flavor olive oil with cloves of garlic, cut in half or left whole, sliced or chopped shallots, and dried hot peppers or pepper flakes. Try these alone or in combination; add some thyme and/or rosemary, and drizzle on pasta, salads, and pizzas.

Makes approximately ⅔ cup

A traditional vinaigrette might not contain the lemon juice, but I like the extra piquancy it adds to a dressing.

1 tablespoon fresh lemon juice
2 tablespoons red wine vinegar
1 small garlic clove, minced or put through
  a press, *or* 1 tablespoon minced shallot (optional)
1 teaspoon Dijon mustard (or more to taste)
1 teaspoon minced fresh tarragon *or* ¼
  teaspoon dried
salt and freshly ground pepper to taste
6 to 8 tablespoons olive oil to taste

1. Stir together everything but the oil, then whisk in the olive oil.

2. Store in the refrigerator if you're not using the vinaigrette within a couple of hours. Taste and adjust the seasonings. This will keep for three days in the refrigerator but is best if used right away.

Low-Fat Olive Oil Vinaigrette

Makes 1 cup

Creamier than a classic vinaigrette, yet containing only half the fat, this dressing has a slightly tart flavor. I use it for many of my salads.

2 tablespoons fresh lemon juice
2 tablespoons vinegar: red wine,
  champagne, or sherry
1 small garlic clove, minced or put through
  a press (optional)
1 teaspoon Dijon mustard
salt and freshly ground pepper to taste
½ cup plain low-fat yogurt
¼ cup olive oil

1. Mix together everything but the olive oil.
2. Whisk in the olive oil or add the olive oil and shake everything together in a jar. Taste and adjust the seasonings. Refrigerate if you're not using the vinaigrette right away. This will keep for a couple of days in the refrigerator, but is best used right away.

CuMiN YoguRT ViNaigReTTe

Makes about 1 cup

Add cumin to a vinaigrette, and suddenly you've got a salad from halfway around the world (India, the Middle East, or Mexico). It's terrific with grain and bean salads. The dressing will keep for three days in the refrigerator but is best used right away.

2 tablespoons wine vinegar or cider vinegar
2 to 3 tablespoons fresh lemon juice
   (to taste)
1 garlic clove, minced or put through a press
1 teaspoon Dijon mustard
½ to 1 teaspoon ground cumin to taste
½ cup plain low-fat yogurt
¼ cup olive oil
salt and freshly ground pepper to taste

1. Mix together the vinegar, lemon juice, garlic, mustard, cumin, and yogurt.
2. Whisk in the oil and season with salt and pepper. Taste and adjust the seasonings.

FooD PRocessoR MayoNNaiSe

Makes 1 cup

**Mayonnaise can be made with all vegetable oil (make sure
you use a mild-flavored one, like sunflower oil) or with
olive oil or, as I like it, with some of each. It's very easy
with a food processor.**

> 1 medium-size egg
> 2 teaspoons wine vinegar
> 1 teaspoon Dijon mustard
> about ½ teaspoon salt (or more to taste)
> ⅓ cup olive oil
> ⅓ cup safflower, canola, *or* sunflower oil
> freshly ground pepper to taste
> 2 tablespoons fresh lemon juice

1. Place the egg, vinegar, mustard, and salt in the food
processor bowl and turn on the processor. Combine the oils
and drizzle ever so slowly, in a thin stream, into the processor as it is running. The mayonnaise will begin to thicken
very quickly and will be quite thick by the time you've
added all of the oil.

2. Add the pepper and lemon juice and combine well.
Transfer to a bowl or jar and refrigerate. The mayonnaise
will keep for about five days in the refrigerator.

Spicy Yogurt-Mayonnaise Dressing

Makes 1½ cups

Tangy, creamy, and just a little bit exotic, this dressing can also serve as a dip for crudités. I particularly like it with grain salads.

½ cup mayonnaise (preferably an olive oil mayonnaise, recipe, page 59, or low-calorie mayonnaise)
¾ cup plain low-fat yogurt
2 to 3 teaspoons curry powder to taste
1½ teaspoons ground cumin
¼ teaspoon chili powder
salt and freshly ground pepper to taste
3 tablespoons fresh lemon juice

1. Combine all the ingredients and mix together well with a whisk or in a food processor. Chill until ready to serve. This will keep for three days in the refrigerator.

Asian Dressing

Whenever you want a salad with the pungent, gingery flavors of the Far East, this is the dressing to use.

> 1 tablespoon fresh lemon juice, fresh lime juice, or cider vinegar
> 2 tablespoons rice wine vinegar or balsamic vinegar
> 1 garlic clove, minced or put through a press
> 2 teaspoons finely minced fresh ginger
> 1 tablespoon tamari or Kikkoman soy sauce
> salt and freshly ground pepper to taste
> ¼ cup dark Chinese sesame oil
> ½ teaspoon hot chili oil or sauce *or* a few dashes of cayenne pepper
> ¼ cup plain low-fat yogurt or buttermilk
> 1 to 2 tablespoons water, depending on how thick you want the dressing to be

1. Combine all the ingredients and blend together well.

2. Store in the refrigerator if you're not using the dressing right away. It will keep for three days.

Garnishes and a Few Basic Salad Additions

Sometimes a salad is so beautiful that it needs no embellishment. Other salads are set off by an extra splash of color — a radish rose or a sprinkling of herbs, a sprig of mint or a bed of frilly lettuce. Some of these extras also contribute texture (like sprouts or sunflower seeds), flavor (herbs, olives) and protein (eggs). Here's a list of suggestions.

Sieved or quartered hard-cooked eggs: Sieved eggs make a subtler, more delicate addition than quartered eggs. You can press quartered hard-cooked eggs through a large garlic press as well as through a sieve.

Chopped fresh herbs and herb sprigs

Alfalfa sprouts

Sunflower seeds

Toasted pine nuts

Black olives (black olives from the Mediterranean are best)

Flower petals from fresh herbs, lavender, citrus, nasturtiums, squash, roses, sunflowers, daylilies, and hibiscus

Cherry tomatoes

Leaf lettuce, for lining bowls and platters

Radish roses

Garlic croutons

Chopped or sliced roasted red peppers

GaRLiC CRouToNS

Not only do these make a great addition to salads and garnish for soups, but they also ensure that any aging loaf of bread that you can still slice will not be wasted. I've never found it necessary to sauté croutons in lots of oil or butter to crisp them up the way the French do. That just makes them greasy. I just toast the bread, rub it with garlic, and cut it to the desired size. This, then, is how you do it:

1. First of all, begin with a good loaf of French bread or whole wheat country bread, not floppy or crumbly bread. Toast thin slices in a toaster or in the oven until crisp. Remove from the heat and rub with a half clove of garlic.
2. If you want a little oil added, brush lightly with olive oil. Cut into small dice, or you can leave baguette slices as they are and cut country bread into 1 to 1½-inch pieces.

Radish Roses

1. To make radish roses, wash the radishes and trim away the tops and the tails if you wish. Using a small sharp knife, cut lengthwise "petals" by cutting slits just inside the red outer skin on three or four sides of the radish (if it's a long, thin radish, you might have room for only three "petals"), cutting from the root end almost down to the stem.
2. Put the radishes in a bowl of cold water and refrigerate. They will open out in a few hours.

METRIC CONVERSION CHART

CONVERSIONS OF OUNCES TO GRAMS

Ounces (oz)	Grams (g)
1 oz	30 g*
2 oz	60 g
3 oz	85 g
4 oz	115 g
5 oz	140 g
6 oz	180 g
7 oz	200 g
8 oz	225 g
9 oz	250 g
10 oz	285 g
11 oz	300 g
12 oz	340 g
13 oz	370 g
14 oz	400 g
15 oz	425 g
16 oz	450 g
20 oz	570 g
24 oz	680 g
28 oz	790 g
32 oz	900 g

*Approximate. To convert ounces to grams, multiply number of ounces by 28.35.

CONVERSIONS OF FAHRENHEIT TO CELSIUS

Fahrenheit	Celsius
170°F	77°C*
180°F	82°C
190°F	88°C
200°F	95°C
225°F	110°C
250°F	120°C
300°F	150°C
325°F	165°C
350°F	180°C
375°F	190°C
400°F	205°C
425°F	220°C
450°F	230°C
475°F	245°C
500°F	260°C
525°F	275°C
550°F	290°C

*Approximate. To convert Fahrenheit to Celsius, subtract 32, multiply by 5, then divide by 9.

CONVERSIONS OF POUNDS TO GRAMS AND KILOGRAMS

Pounds (lb)	Grams (g); kilograms (kg)
1 lb	450 g*
1¼ lb	565 g
1½ lb	675 g
1¾ lb	800 g
2 lb	900 g
2½ lb	1,125 g; 1¼ kg
3 lb	1,350 g
3½ lb	1,500 g; 1½ kg
4 lb	1,800 g
4½ lb	2 kg
5 lb	2¼ kg
5½ lb	2½ kg
6 lb	2¾ kg
6½ lb	3 kg
7 lb	3¼ kg
7½ lb	3½ kg
8 lb	3¾ kg
9 lb	4 kg
10 lb	4½ kg

*Approximate. To convert pounds into kilograms, multiply number of pounds by 453.6.

CONVERSIONS OF QUARTS TO LITERS

Quarts (qt)	Liters (L)
1 qt	1 L*
1½ qt	1½ L
2 qt	2 L
2½ qt	2½ L
3 qt	2¾ L
4 qt	3¾ L
5 qt	4¾ L
6 qt	5½ L
7 qt	6½ L
8 qt	7½ L
9 qt	8½ L
10 qt	9½ L

*Approximate. To convert quarts to liters, multiply number of quarts by 0.95.